A Tafiti Kids Adventure

The Secret History of Popular Symbols Used in Everyday Life

An Interactive Coloring Workbook

Kimberly Gordon

5D Media Publishing

www.5dMedia.org | support@5Dmedia.org | PO Box 10586 Westbury, NY 11590

Ordering Information: Quantity sales. Special discounts are available on quantity purchases by corporations, associations, and others. For details, contact the publisher at the address above.

Orders by U.S. trade bookstores and wholesalers. Please contact Big Distribution: orders@5dmedia.org or visit www.5DMedia.org.

Printed in the United States of America

The Secret History of Popular Symbols Used in Everyday Life: An Interactive Coloring Workbook / **Kimberly Gordon**

ISBN-13: 978-0-9989217-9-2

First Edition

Warning! You have unlocked the Tablet of Hidden Secrets. You can now travel back in time to unlock top mysteries of the world. The tablet is powerful and must be protected. It contains information even your teachers have not learned. Are you ready?

Write your name on the Tablet of Hidden Secretes below to become an official Tafiti Kid. Then, flip the page to begin your first adventure.

(Your Name)

Assignment One: Investigate Symbols you see every day but do not know what they mean

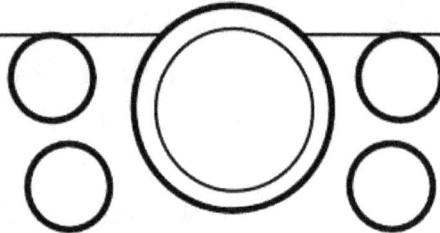

What Are Symbols?

Hand gestures and visual images known as signs were the primary way ancient humans communicated before developing a spoken language. Signs have existed throughout history for everything including plants, feelings, and even parts of the body.

Signs that have a bigger meaning are known as symbolic images, or symbols. They represent ideas and universal connections based on emotions and feelings. What they symbolize grows and changes over time.

Did you know "Tafiti" means "Do Research" in Swahili?

The most powerful symbols represent abstract concepts and emotions and have existed since ancient times. These same symbols continue to be valuable today. Some are universally understood and have shared meanings between most people around the world. Other symbols represent something different in each culture.

Symbolic images are often a combination of signs. The most basic and oldest signs are the circle, the square, the triangle, the arrow, and the cross. These signs have been merged to create countless new symbols.

While Sign Language still exists in various forms, several hand gestures have developed into symbols with deeper meanings. Secret

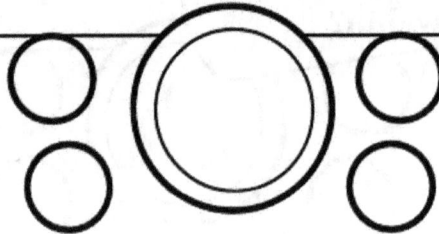

messages have been included in portraits and paintings for thousands of years using hand gesture symbols and symbolic images.

Did you know that symbols are everywhere? They are in company logos, in our favorite movies, and even on country flags. Many of them were discovered on ancient art, pottery, textiles and even quilts from prehistoric civilizations. It is important to understand the history of these symbols to understand why they are being used. Follow us to learn about some of the oldest and most popular Symbols on earth!

Go to the next page to
Read, Color and Learn
with us.
Then, create your own
symbol to add to the
collection.

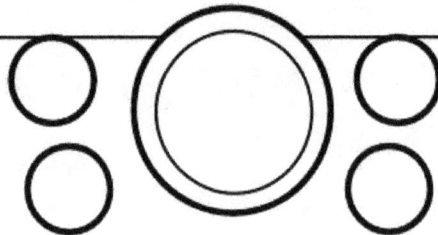

DIKENGA COSMOGRAM

The first symbol you may not recognize at first in its original form. The Dikenga Cosmogram has been found in prehistoric cave paintings in central Africa and is believed to be the most ancient symbolic image.   Many powerful ancient and modern symbols were created based on it.

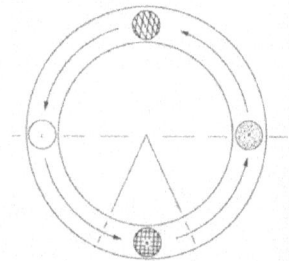

The Dikenga symbolic image was created by observing the sun as it traveled from east to west in the sky to represent an ancient Bântu-Kôngo African belief system about birth, life, death, and rebirth.

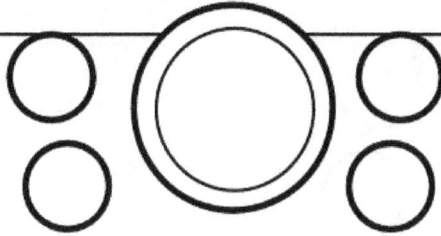

Dikenga symbolic images vary from simple to complex. They all include four points that represent movement between the four positions of the Sun. The Bântu-Kôngo people call these points "dingo-y-dingo," or "coming and going from the center."

It is believed that this symbol only reveals its true meaning to those who can understand. The Dikenga has so many symbols within it, that there are an unlimited number of meanings someone can get from looking at it. They all tell a story.

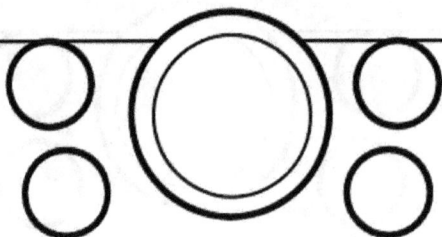

The arrows can signify the circle of life, the energy of the universe, obtaining knowledge, cycles in nature, and history repeating itself. The cross in the middle can represent a moral compass. There is also an idea of the world of the living and the spirit world being separated by water.

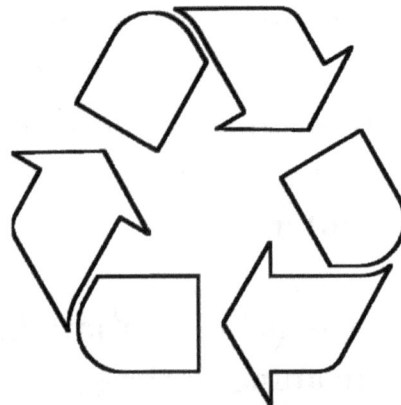

The Dikenga Cosmogram symbol was carried from the continent of Africa in the hearts and minds of enslaved Africans to the United States, where it has been discovered on many artifacts.

The Dikenga is so powerful that it has a different meaning to everyone who looks at it. What do you see?

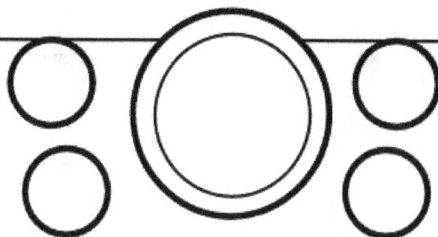

THE RAISED FIST

The raised fist gesture has been used as a symbol of strength, unity and defiance since the first human civilization.

In ancient Mesopotamian art the Goddess of War, Ishtar, is depicted with a Raised Fist salute. With one arm in the air and a clenched fist, Ishtar appears in artifacts standing strong while resisting violence. This gesture has appeared in art depicting war and resistance ever since.

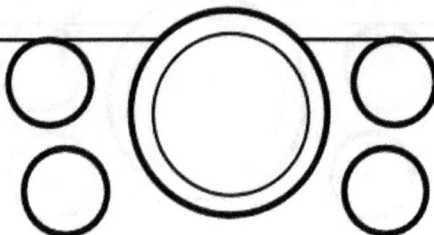

The symbolic image symbol became popular in 1917 when it was used by the Industrial Workers Labor Union as a logo while resisting capitalism.

Soon Raised Fist images and salutes were being used by groups that felt oppressed around the world.

In the 1960s the Black Fist symbol became popular as a logo for Black American pride and the **Black Power** movement. **Both the logo and salute were used to defy** civil rights violations.

Since then the Raised Fist continued to flourish as a powerful symbol of social revolution.

Symbols cannot be defined. But we can learn about their history to create our own meanings.
What does this symbol mean to you?

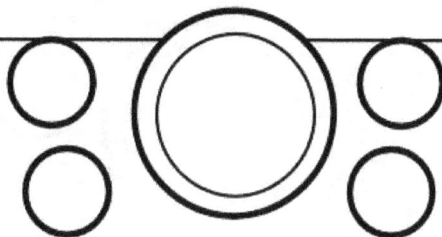

THE TREE OF LIFE

Trees have been respected throughout history, because human beings could not exist without trees providing us oxygen to breath. Symbolic images of trees have symbolized life, death, good, and evil.

The Tree of Life symbol originated in Babylonian mythology as a magical tree that grew in the center of paradise. Ancient Egypt, Iran, Mesopotamia and Urartu also had their own version of a Tree of Life symbol.

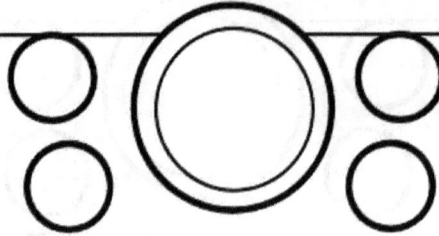

The Tree of Life Symbol remains sacred today. It is mentioned in the Bible in the Book of Genesis as the Tree of Paradise that grows within the Garden of Eden and is the source of eternal life.

In Buddhism, Buddha reaches enlightenment under the Bhodi-tree, which is believed to be the Tree of Enlightenment.

In Islam, it is the Tree of Immortality from which Adam and Eve ate.

In Judaism, The Tree of Knowledge stands in the center of a fruitful garden planted by Yahweh and sustains and nourishes life.

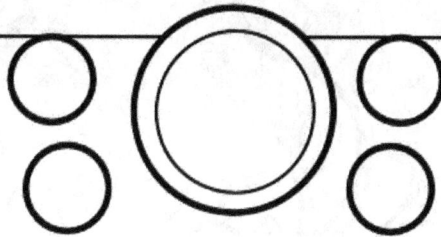

Symbolic images of trees do not always look the same, but they usually include a large tree with branches and roots. Sometimes the roots are exceptionally long, and there is a circle around the symbol.

The Tree of Life symbol remains strong today and is used frequently. One example is the Family Tree, which symbolizes a connection to ancestors that share roots - the tree grows to give life to every new generation. In popular culture Tree of Life symbolic characters are used in movies and television shows, including Avatar, Harry Potter and Pocahontas.

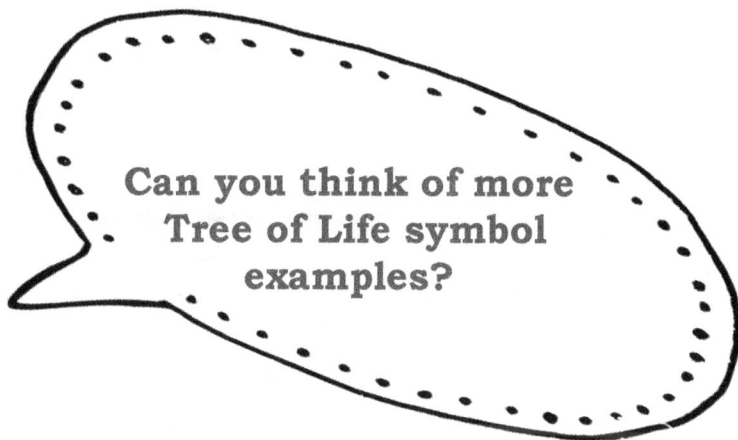

Can you think of more Tree of Life symbol examples?

Try to Create your own symbolic image for the phrase in the box below

Hard Work

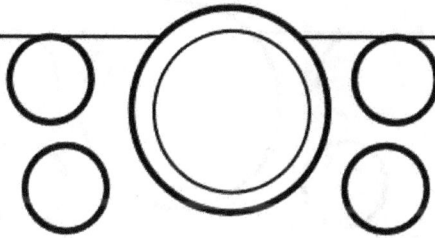

THE WEDJAT EYE

Universally, symbolic images of the eye are depictions of a deity watching over the people. **They also operate as a reminder to pay attention, be observant, mindful, aware and present.**

The oldest known eye symbol originated as the Egyptian hieroglyphic for the cobra Goddess of protection Wadjet. The symbolic image of her left eye represented protection and taking action to ancient Egyptians.

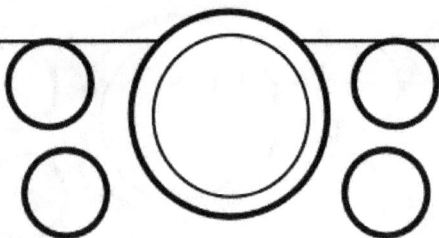

The God Horus later became known as the most popular Egyptian God in the world through the myth of Isis and Osiris.

He was known as the protector of Egypt, so the Wadjet eye became more popularly known as The Eye of Horus.

As the Eye of Horus the Symbol grew to represent sacrifice, healing, divine intervention, regeneration, wholeness, prosperity and protection. It remains the most well-known Egyptian Symbol today.

The right eye of Wadjet grew into a symbol known as the Eye of Ra. It symbolizes protection, but through power, violence, or a destructive force.

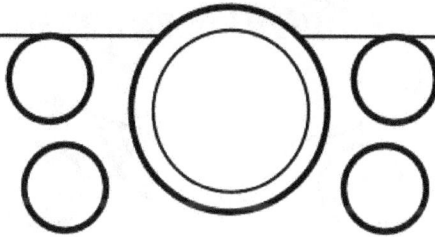

The Wadjet eye design is made up of six individual signs, with each one representing one of the six senses: smell, sight, thought, hearing, taste, and touch. Each sign is strategically placed and sized as an exact replica of the pineal gland inside the brain.

The Eye of Providence, from Judaism and Christianity, is a symbolic design represented by an eye placed inside of a triangle. The triangle is its own symbol that symbolizes a trinity. In Christianity it represents the Father, Son, and Holy Spirit. Sometimes there are rays

of light surrounding the triangle to further represent the connection to a higher power. All variations symbolize God, or a higher power, as all-seeing and always watching over us.

The Eye of Providence symbol is included on the Great Seal of the United States and can be seen on a US one-dollar bill.

Shiva, one of the gods of the Hindu trinity, is always depicted with a third eye on their forehead, aligned with the crown chakra. In Buddhism, the Buddha himself is referred to as the 'Eye of the World' or the 'Eye of Truth'.

6

Look at a US $1 Bill.
Draw the symbols
you see below.

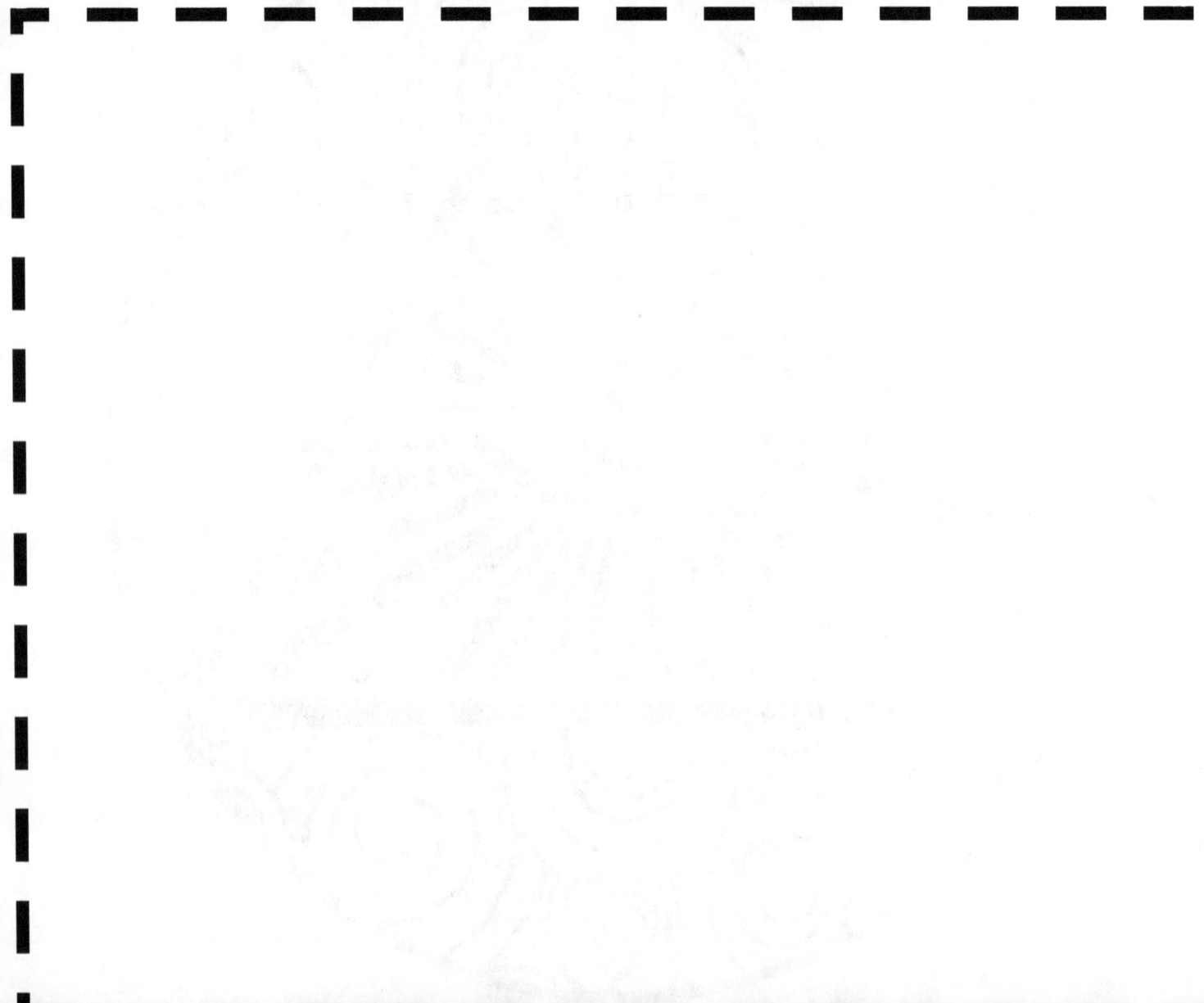

What do these symbols on the US $1 bill mean to you?

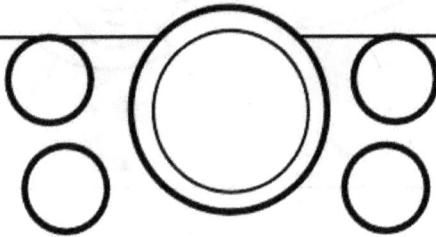

TAIJITU

Taijitu means great pole. The oldest known version of the Taijitu image was designed over 2,600 years ago in China based on the visual created by a pole used to tell time by monitoring the changing shadows formed when sun light hit. Taijitu symbolic images were placed on these poles to symbolize the Ancient African Law of Opposites and perfect balance.

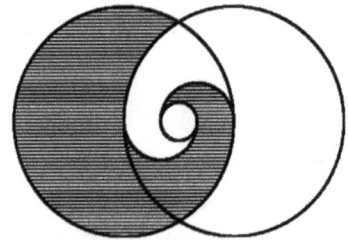

According to Ancient African Myths that are 20,000 years old, *the sky* Gods Neter and Netert work together to create balance in the

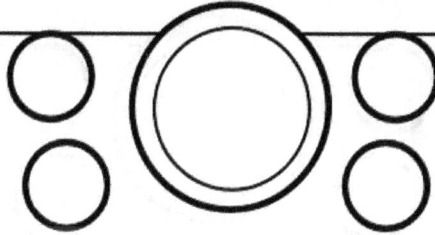

universe. The original Taijitu symbol incorporated even light and dark portions within a circle.

The light symbolized the God Neter, representing the time of year where the days were longer than the night. The darker symbolized the Goddess Netert, representing the periods of the year when the nights were longer. This displayed that there could not be day without night, or shadows without light.

The Taijutu symbol was cultivated when the Tao philosophy was born and blossomed into the Taoism religion in China. The two sides were then called Yin and Yang.

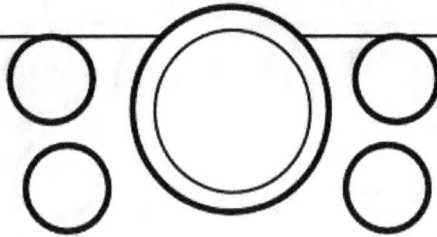

The Chinese created many symbolic images to represent Yin and Yang over hundreds of years. One version became extremely popular and universally accepted and understood.

They began with a circle, which represented Wiji, a symbol representing the universe. Then they used two swirls, one light and one dark, that swirled into each other. Near the center of each one they placed a dot of the opposite color.

The dark sections represent Yin – femininity, water, earth, moon and nighttime, and is considered passive, cold, soft, yielding and wet.

The light sections represent Yang - masculinity, fire, sin, sky, and daytime, and is considered aggressive, hot, hard and dry. The light signifies delusion, while the dark signifies enlightenment.

In the 1960s the modern Yin Yang symbolic image became popular around the word. In this variation the halves look more like fish swimming in opposite directions head to tail, in a circle. Each section contains a small circle belonging to the other. This symbol is now universally understood and recognized to represent opposites working together creating balance in the circle of life.

In Taijitu symbols separate parts work together to accomplish a goal. **They support and complete each other.**

What are some examples of opposites that work together?

_____

_____

_____

_____

_____

_____

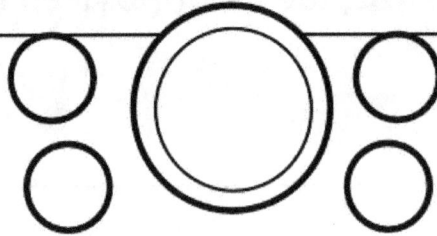

PEACE SIGN

This popular modern universal symbol was designed in 1958 by artist Gerald Holtom for the British Campaign for Nuclear Disarmament, a company that wanted to get rid of all Nuclear Weapons around the world. Holtom used other symbols to create his. Can you guess what they are?

He began with a circle. The circle symbol has had many meanings throughout history.

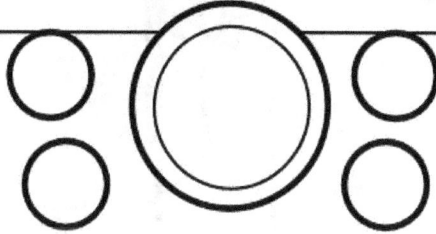

In ancient Native American symbols, the circle signifies the world, family ties, closeness and protection. The circle has no breaks and cannot be broken. **In the Hindu culture, a circle represents wisdom.**

Inside the circle Holtom used letters from the semaphore alphabet. These letters are formed by stretching arms out and holding flags in different positions that represent each letter of the alphabet. The two short lines are a "N" and the long center line is a "D," representing the words "Nuclear Disarmament."

This symbol is now a popular idea for peace.

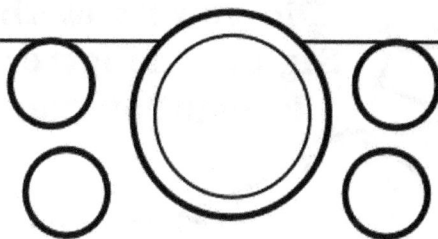

V SIGN

Hand gestures have been used for nonverbal communication since the beginning of human history. The V Sign was originally seen around the world as a symbol of resistance. For at least 500 years the hand gesture extending the index and middle fingers in the air with knuckles turned out was used as a sign of disrespect. It was commonly used to tease or intimidate.

During World War II a V for Victory campaign began where the letter V was used as a symbolic image against Nazi rule.

Did you know the V Sign is the letter "V" in sign language?

In 1941 UK Prime Minister Winston Churchill began holding the V sign hand gesture, extending the index and middle fingers in the air with his palm out, as a salute. Soon all allies, including the United States, began utilizing both the hand gesture and symbolic images of the hand gesture for the same purpose.

This effort led to African Americans adopting the Double V Symbol, with an additional V symbolizing Victory over oppression and inequalities faced by African American soldiers and civilians by the United States. Many historians believe the Double V campaign lead to the 1960s civil rights protests.

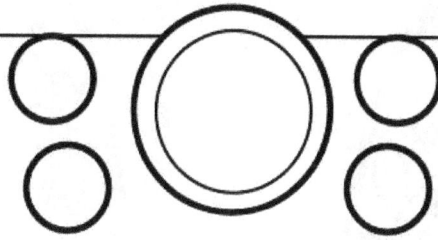

Since the war, the V Sign has become very popular in Japan where it is known as pīsu sain, or peace sign. It is a widely used hand gesture and pose in photographs used to show peaceful intentions.

Now that we have unlocked information about popular symbols, it is time for you to create your own symbolic image. Then let us know what it means to you on the following page.

Understand other people may view your symbol and see something totally different. And that is alright.

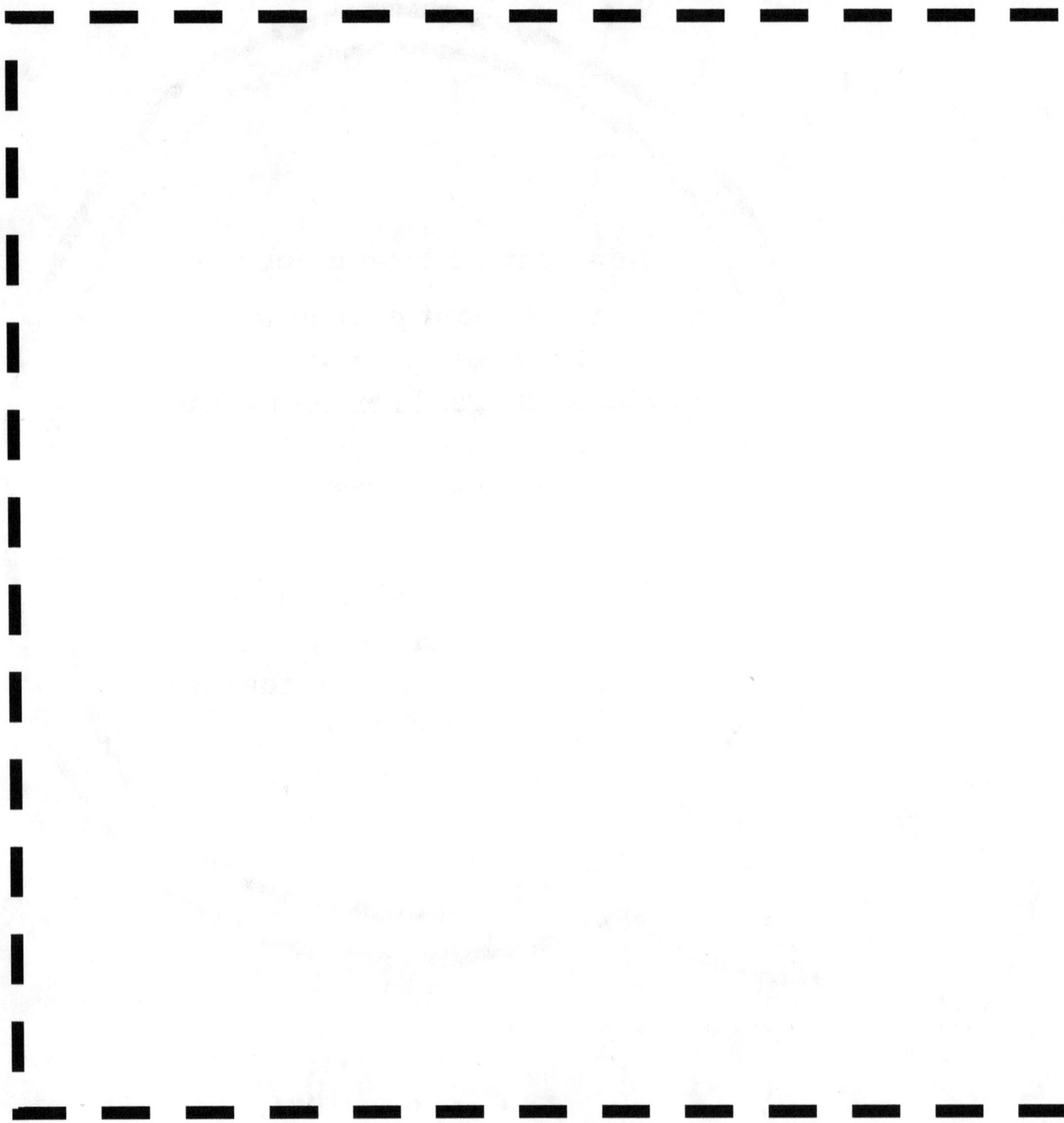

_____

(Name Your Symbol)

_____

_____

_____

_____

_____

_____

Congratulations on creating your symbol!

If you are interested in wearing your symbol as a sticker, tee shirt or hat, visit:

https://www.5dmedia.org/collections .

To join us on more Tafiti Kid adventures, visit:
https://www.5dmedia.org/collections/TafitiKids

SOURCES

Biederman, Hans. *Dictionary of Symbolism: Cultural Icons and the Meanings Behind Them.* Meridian, 1994.

Clark, R.T.R. : Myth and Symbol in Ancient Egypt, Thames & Hudson - London, 1959.

Cotterell, Arthur, 'Isthar.' *A Dictionary of World Mythology*, New York, G. P. Putman's Sons, 1980, p. 36

Frutiger, Adrian. *Signs and Symbols: Their Design and Meaning.* Van Nostrand Reinhold, 1989.

Fu-Kiau, **Kimbwandende Kia Bunseki.** African Cosmology of the Bantu-Kongo: Tying the Spiritual Knot, Principles of Life & Living. Athelia Henrietta Press, 2001

Gundaker, Grey. "The Kongo Cosmogram in Historical Archaeology and the Moral Compass of Dave the Potter." *Historical Archaeology*, vol. 45, no. 2, 2011, pp. 176–183. *JSTOR*, www.jstor.org/stable/23070096

Harper, Prudence and Joan Aruz. "Assyrian Origins: Discoveries at Ashur on the Tigris : Antiquities in the Vorderasiatisches Museum, Berlin." Metropolitan Museum of Art, 1995.

Inman, Thomas and John Newton. *Ancient Pagan and Modern Christian Symbolism.* J.W. Boulton, 1875.

Jaeger, Stefan. "A Geomedical Approach to Chinese Medicine: The Origin of the Yin-Yang Symbol." In "*Recent Advances in Theories and Practice of Chinese Medicine.*" Ed. HaixueKuang. IntechOpen, 2011.

Rucker, Rudy. *Infinity and the Mind: The Science and Philosophy of the Infinite.* Princeton University Press, 2004.

Thompson, Robert Farris. *Art and Altars of Africa and the African Americas (African Art).*Prestel, 1993.
Thompson, Robert Farris. *Flash of the Spirit: African and Afro-American Art and Philosophy.* Vintage, 1984.

Wahlman, Maude Southwell. *Signs and Symbols: African Images in African American Quilts.* Tinwood Books, 2001.

Washburn, Patrick S. "The Pittsburgh *Courier's* Double V Campaign in 1942." American Journalism, 1986, pg 73-86, https://doi.org/10.1080/08821127.1986.10731062

Woodrow, Ralph. *Babylon Mystery Religion: Ancient and Modern.* Ralph Woodrow, *1966*

ABOUT THE AUTHOR

Kimberly Gordon is an award-winning author and mixed media artist from New York City.

She was first recognized for her work when she received the National Gold Key Art Award in Washington, DC for a Mixed Media Collage Self Portrait. The piece was also on display at the Smithsonian Art Museum.

Kimberly later received the Maya Angelou award for Academic Excellence for her written and documentary film work in Africana Studies. Since then she has published several books, and mixed media art pieces.

For information about the author and her work, visit 5dMedia.org.

Instagram: @KimberlyGordonBooks

Twitter: @KimberlyGordon_

www.ingramcontent.com/pod-product-compliance
Lightning Source LLC
Chambersburg PA
CBHW080602030426
42336CB00019B/3307

9 780998 921792